The Revelations of 30

Porsha O. M. George

BookLeaf Publishing

India | USA | UK

Presentation by *BookLeaf Publishing*

Web: www.bookleafpub.com

E-mail: info@bookleafpub.com

ISBN: 9789360948825

First edition 2024

This work of art is dedicated to my mother, may she rest well! I thank you for giving me life! To my grandmother! Thank you for covering me with love and wisdom! To my dearest Zahyd! Thank you for nurturing my voice and caring for me!

The Light's Affirmations

I AM loved!
I AM healed!

I AM creative!
I AM financially independent!

I AM in sync and aligned!
I AM strong!

I AM faithful!
I AM loyal!

I AM Divine!
I AM intentional!

I AM compassionate!
I AM a leader!

I AM a resourceful genius!
I AM worthy!

I release all that no longer serves me!
I AM walking in my purpose!

I AM shining without restraint!

I AM prosperous!

I AM free from all judgment!
I AM free from all guilt and shame!

I AM free from toxic masculinity!
I AM free from toxic femininity!

I COME FROM SOURCE!
I HAVE ALL THAT I NEED!
I CAN DO ALL THINGS!

I AM GROUNDED!
I AM PEACE!
I AM WHOLE!

I LET GO!
I LET GOD!

ALL THINGS WORK IN MY FAVOR!
ASÈ!

Porsha:
A feminine name of German origin, meaning
offering!

As a woman of spiritual wealth and wisdom, I
offer these words to you!

Dear Mama

I forgive you and I love you
Help me understand.

Why you left me here alone
To navigate this land.

Pushing forward my Beloved
Help see me through.

Show me what my eyes can't see
I depend on you.

Dear momma,
I pray that you can hear my voice

Guide me to a better way
If I make the wrong choice.

I only hope that healing me will somehow heal
you too.

Shed your light on anything I believe I can not
do.

Enhance my wisdom so I can teach my niece.

Provide us comfort on your absence
and restore our peace.

I make the best of my experience here in this
life.

Staying prayed up, streets filled with strife.

There are days when I wonder why you kept me
alive.

To the answer, one day I will truly arrive.

Young me, pacing through the halls you walked.

At 6, reminiscing on the times we talked.

Feeling like a young you when you were in your
prime.

What a way to grow up, questioning yourself all
the time.

Walking by faith not by sight.

A lineage of greatness! Yea, that's right!

Hope to see you in my dreams at night!

Continue to shield me and protect my light!

5

Dear mama…
I love you…

The Money Mantra

I manifest with intention.

Working on my retention.

Creating a lifestyle they can't help but mention.

On a money making mission.

Quadruple the digits.

You can see the grind happening,

I'll holla when I'm finished!

I'm bossin', flossin' and saucin'. Okay!
I want it done right, I've got to do it my way!

Where yo confidence at?

Where yo mindset at?

How long you plan to focus on "bad" days
and those setbacks?

Get grounded!

Get realigned, and back on track!

Ain't you ready for a real meal, put down them snacks!

You've got to count it up, elevate, calm your nerves, find solutions and bounce it!

Work your passive income, accomplish your goals, and don't make no announcements!

Union

A woman with intellect.
Inner peace.
Goddess.
Air.
Fire.
Earth.
Water.
Purpose.
Consciousness.
Entertains for a moment.
Entertains the notion of a shared space.
A shared sacred spiritual space. With a man.
A man who is brutally honest yet kind.
Kind to her. Kind to the woman.
The woman with light.
With darkness.
Awareness.
Love.
Love for herself.
Therefore love for him.
Love for her mirror. The strength in her.
Magnifies connected to him. The depth.
What they are individually. Magnificent.
Together, they are a muse. A fuse.
Untouchable. Bold. Peaceful.

In her arms he resets.
In his arms she rests.
Leaders. Creatives.
A safe space.
Ultimate.
Resting.
Place.

Misunderstood

It is said that the key is in communication. I've found that comprehension is what makes or breaks a strong foundation. See, you can have a conversation all day long but if you're not committed to gaining an understanding you won't quite get to the root of what's actually wrong. The definition of effective is being successful in producing an intended result. How can you get to the root when certain aspects of your truth remain in the vault? Were you completely transparent and they still didn't hear you? Maybe they are listening to respond and have some inner work to do. Some conversations may not play out exactly as they should. Without comprehension, it is easy to be misunderstood!

Born Again

Up and down.
In and out.

Born again!

Wondering when and where the cycle ends?

Journeys are ongoing, there's no destination!

Thought you'd hit rock bottom and busting
through the ceiling.

Can and Can't can feel the same if you ain't
really listening!

History repeats until you learn the lessons.

Heal your heart and take a breath so you don't
blockblessings!

Forgive yourself and recommit; start again!
It's okay to rest but do not quit; It's not the end!

No more worries, it's above me now!
It's in the wind!

Two wrongs don't make a right, tap into your
consciousness!

It's okay to be yourself!
Change starts within!

Vibe, presence, mood!
An experience!

I was divinely created and I will ascend!
To be reborn, renewed to begin again!

Key 2 My Lock

Cross the ocean, bend the block, for you I will.
The key to my lock.

A joining of 2. 1 mind body and soul. The
woman he craves and seeks to make whole.

A frequent surge. A synergy of greatness. Flying
high altitudes, with you my heart is weightless.

Infinite supply. You've become my natural high.
Something so unique it's not to be categorized.

Walking a fine line between the spiritual and
reality. I wish I could have this forever in full
totality.

Awakening my senses, the ones you can't see.
When we think of one another it's instant
telepathy.

Expansive by nature. Never seen anything like
this. We evolve together quickly because we're
intentionally in the midst.

We honor each other, that's why it works. Love is designed to heal. It was not intended to hurt.

A spark in our connection that goes back before existence. I am blessed in this experience to be present as a witness.

Creation in real time, setting the stage for what's to come. Building our empire, coming second to none.

Joining as one. 1 mind body and soul. It's him I yearn to touch. His hands I need to hold.

I love you. I feel like I could never say it enough. It was divine timing and favor not pure luck.

A bond to not be broken, the match to my sock. I will always hold space for the key to my lock.

Internalized

To whom it may concern:

The words poured into you, wrapped with ill intentions, are not who you are!

The boxes of societal norms are not becoming of you!

The expression of your experiences has purpose!

Expression by force drives me to the center explosion.

I'm a recovering people pleaser; I no longer support that notion.

Continuous internal conflict.
Your opinions and my uniqueness.

Exhausted by this cycle,
I'm ready for a new sequence.

You want me to follow your rules?
Make this a safe space.

If you can't accept my request,
I surely rest my case!

I call my power back to restore my spiritual
health!

Internalizing a negative feeling about self is to
diminish the true value of your wealth!

Roots

For beautiful leaves, I must nurture my roots.

The strength of my tree, lies in the roots.

My soil indeed, impacts the roots.

As I water the seed, I encourage the roots.

The oxygen received, flows through my roots.

My stride, my longevity, begins with my roots.

The fruit on my tree, which began with a seed, required my growth to meet every need. When walking by faith, there's no need to plead. I operate in obedience, allowing Spirit to lead. I am resilient up top because of the firm planting of my feet. Tending to the roots of my soul, has become my peace!

An Empty Cup

Why is your cup empty?

What's in your cup is for you!

Pouring from an empty cup is not what you do!

The overflow in your saucer is for you to share!

Giving from the prosperity of your fruit is how you express nurture and care!

Your self preservation depends on your retention of this!

The quality of your offerings should be wrapped in bliss!

You can only do this from overflow not from depletion!

Never pour from an empty cup!

Not for any reason!

Synergy

NURTURE..

A held hand..
A kissed lip..
A solid man..
A steady grip..

INTIMACY..

The connection of our souls.
That travels through the spark in the eyes.
Down the small of my back.
Evaporation up my spine.

WATER..

Your energy pouring over me…
Condensation.
The colder parts of my heart warming up…
Sublimation.
Warming up for only you…
Infiltration.
Sacred, holy and divine…
Consecration.

MANIFESTATION.

I called to you and for you to appear...
It tripped me up and stifled my fear...
Taking me to a mirror where I examined
myself...
Feeling the love I desired radiating outside of
myself...
Mmhm
A muse.
Mmhmm
A fuse.
The energy there you left in my heart I'll never
lose.

Sublime

The work being done.

The work that's bearing early fruit.

Powerful essence that flows from the seed,
through the roots!

The fruit that can only be seen from heightened
frequencies.

Working with what you have been given and
making every effort to protect your sovereignty!

Seen in other dimensions.
Might you tap further into the spirit.

Further into your spiritual nature.
Where you have to close your eyes to hear it!

So intune that what you start, you always finish.

Keeping in mind you are a spiritual being having
a human experience!

So confident that we know the desire is the
foretelling of success.

Abundance is becoming of you. Embrace your
fortitude being put to the test!

For you are powerful, sublime, divine,
purposeful and poised.

A force who understands they are massive
enough to fill any void!

As to be gentle when necessary and firm when
called.
Might we do the work, intentionally!

Signed,
—Goddess, the daughter of Allah!

In the Eye of the Beholder

There is beauty in the simplicity of life!

The tree that saved me from the rain.
The Friend that wiped tears and eased pain.

There is beauty in the simplicity of life!

The flower growing out of the concrete.
The sound of a baby's first heartbeat.

There is beauty in the simplicity of life!

The birds chirping on a hot summer day.
The abundance of flowers that bloom in May.

There is beauty in the simplicity of life!

The breeze that cooled me down.
The butterfly landing on the ground.

There is beauty in the simplicity of life!

The deep breath and tea or coffee in the
morning.

The financial blessing you received without
warning.

There is beauty in the simplicity of life!

The ocean and its waves.
The moon in every phase.

There is beauty in the simplicity of life!

Self Care

Took myself to lunch and bought a new fit.

Replaced my chair with a throne as I needed a
new place to sit.

An upgraded attitude, God does all things well.

The spoken affirmations that lifted me up out of
my shell.

A massage to my shoulders as I've been tense.

Balanced boundaries, not a wall, more so a
fence.

Walks through nature, the wisdom in the wind I
received.

Witnessing the presence of the Fibonacci
sequence in the flowers, sea shells and trees.

The candle I lit as I brushed my hair.

I will always make time for myself, my self
care!

Legacy

My work ethic will enhance lives for centuries.

Endless creativity fueled by epiphanies.

The force and drive I spark in others.

I encourage free thinkers, they are not to be smothered.

Teaching financial literacy to children.

Vowing that philanthropy and humanitarianism will be my mission.

Building lifelong connections and generational wealth.

Teaching importance of mental, physical, emotional and spiritual health.

Providing education on excellent credit. Strategies on understanding the human mind so that all access is properly vetted.

Designing a massive blueprint for
comprehending computers and coding.

The greatness of my legacy, rest assured, it's
loading!

Perception

Everybody knows what I've been through!
So they say...

Everybody knows how it feels to wear my
shoes...

How are you so comfortable talking to me, about
me, when you haven't gotten to know me?

I really would go there with you but I don't have
time!

I wish that you could understand me but you're
so blind!

Because of your perception of me, my gears you
grind!

I would explain myself but I'm in my prime!

People's perception,
It'll drive you up a wall!

Not minding their business, will be their
downfall!

Before you fix your lips to judge me at all, beware the stones you pick, living in your glass house...

I am the human representation of the glass half empty, glass half full theory. How you view me is based totally on your opinion and will not dictate how I live my life!

Break the Chain

I will not become who I came from.
Break the curse!

I will not become the environment that raised
me.
Break the cycle!

For the longevity of my existence, this is vital!

How I was groomed is no longer my inner voice.
Deeper Healing!

I deserve to have my voice be heard.
Deeper awareness!

Boundaries are necessary, no more being
careless!

Freedom in this instance is subjective.
I've been released now!

The bruising from the chains will hurt.
I'm keeping them off anyhow!

If they don't understand, you cannot force them.
How many times have you sacrificed to go out
on the limb?

A revelation of this kind is jarring at the roots.
Like trying to breathe with lungs covered in
soot!

Heavy is the head that wears the crown indeed!
With the revelations of this journey, my peace is
truly guaranteed!

Phoenix

I've been protecting my energy, give me 6 feet, no corona.

Not playing with my future, nor my destiny, yeah I'm on one.

Manifesting financial freedom, I'm a leader, a young wise one.

Dripping Divinity daily, God's soldier, I can't be undone.

I'm tied up like a shoestring, running in this race.

I do my thang on the daily, because I'm coming in first place.

You got something to say to me? Address it in my face.

No bad energy consuming my space.

Much like the Phoenix, I rise!

Out of the ashes, like a lotus of the muddiest
waters!

Again and again, I triumph!
Again and again, I rise!

I am resilient, resilient indeed, I AM!